Contents

1. The School Buildings — 2
2. The Playground and Playing Field — 5
3. Points of the Compass — 9
4. Wild Places — 12
5. By the School — 14

The School Buildings

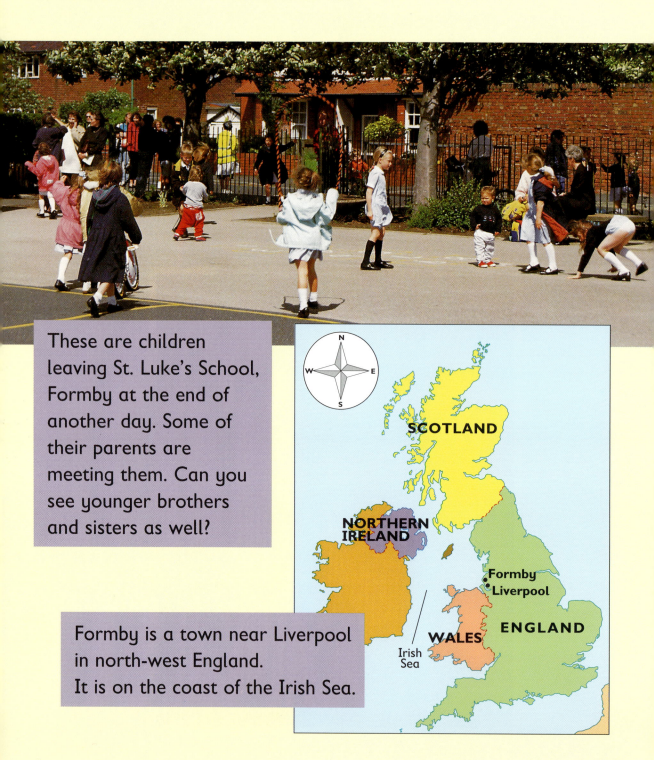

These are children leaving St. Luke's School, Formby at the end of another day. Some of their parents are meeting them. Can you see younger brothers and sisters as well?

Formby is a town near Liverpool in north-west England. It is on the coast of the Irish Sea.

The school was built by people who went to St. Luke's Church. Local people called it "the little church in the sandhills."

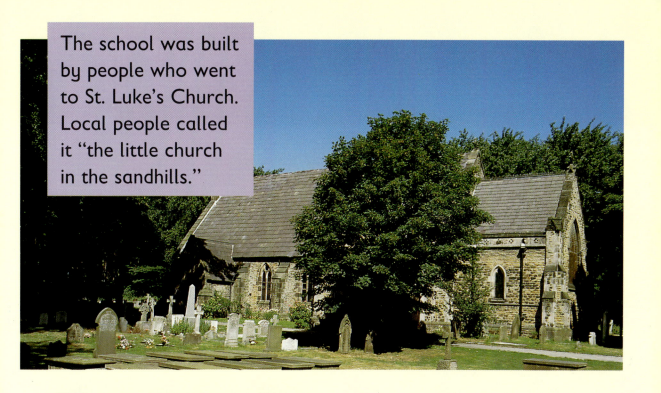

The school was built in 1911. The old building is still used.

Some of the school buildings are old and some are new. As more and more people came to live in Formby, the school grew bigger.
New classrooms were added.

Today some of the children are taught in mobile classrooms.
Is your school old or new, or a mixture of both?

The Playground and Playing Field

Like most of Formby, St. Luke's school is built on flat, sandy ground. Sandy soils are dry, and the grass on the playing field can quickly turn yellow in dry weather. The grass is easily worn away.

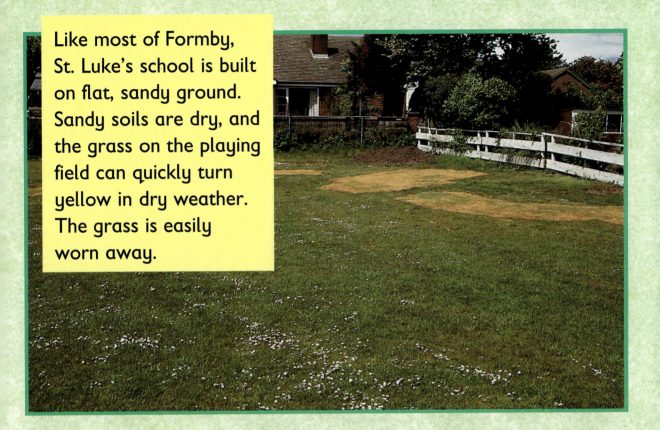

Can you see where new grass seed has been sown?

The children have two areas to play on. The playing field is grass and the playground is tarmac.
After it rains, the water drains quickly into the sandy soil.
Water stays longer on the tarmac playground, as it cannot soak in.

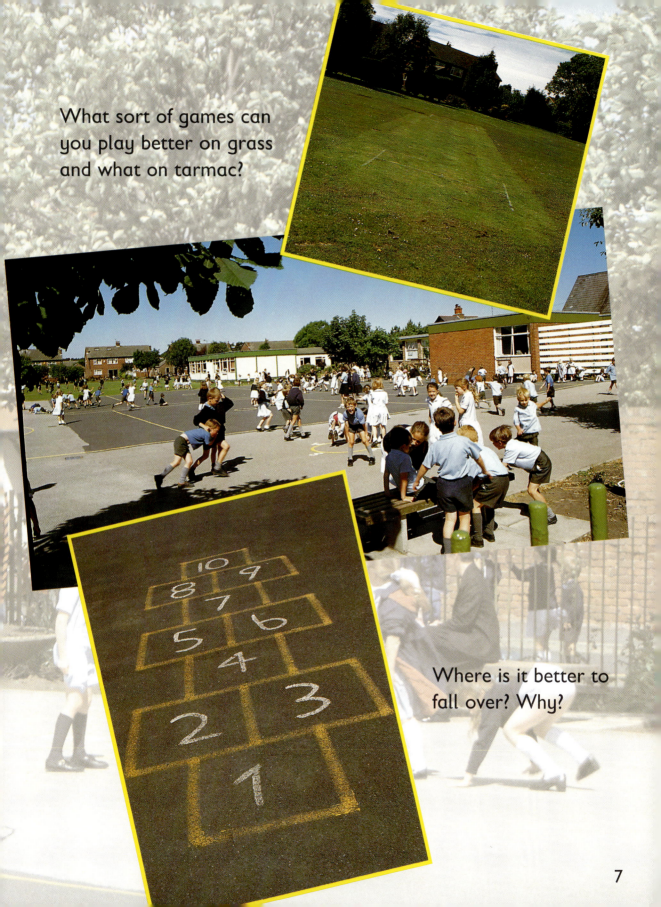

What sort of games can you play better on grass and what on tarmac?

Where is it better to fall over? Why?

7

On sunny days, people make shadows, and buildings and trees make shade. It is cooler in the shade.
Do you like being in the sun or shade on a hot day? Why?

Points of the Compass

The main points of the compass have been drawn on the tarmac of the playground. These show the sides of the school face different directions.

How does the weather-cock on the roof show the direction in which the wind is blowing?

There is a different view in each direction from the school grounds.

NORTH, EAST, SOUTH, WEST, which is the view that you like best? Why?

Wild Places

In the school grounds are wild places where lots of plants grow. In this area there is a pond, with different sorts of plants. In the spring it has tadpoles.

The school paths and welcome areas have tidy plant borders.

There are seats where parents can wait for their children at the end of the school day.

By the School

This is a drawing of the buildings around St. Luke's school. Most of them are houses with their own gardens.

These are some of the houses on Jubilee Road. The school is on Jubilee Road.

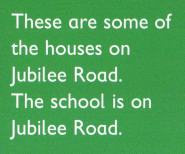

Some houses are small and some are big. Some are old and some are new. The walls and roofs are made of different materials.

Index

borders   13
compass   9, 10, 11
directions   10, 11
Formby   2, 4, 5
gardens   14
grass   5, 7
houses   14, 15
Irish Sea   2
Jubilee Road   15
Liverpool   2
mobile classrooms   4
parents   2, 13
paths   13
plants   12, 13
playground   6, 9
playing field   5, 6
pond   12
rain   6
St. Luke's Church   3
St. Luke's School   2, 5, 14
school buildings   4
school grounds   10
shadow   8
soil   5, 6
spring   12
sun   8
tadpoles   12
tarmac   6, 7, 9
weather cock   9
welcome area   13
wild places   12
wind   9